BEYOND
PANINI

© 2005 Silverback Books, Inc.

Project Editor: Lisa M. Tooker

Translator: Christie Tam

Editor: Lynda Zuber Sassi

Design & Typography: Elizabeth M. Watson

Layout & Production: Patty Holden

Photography: Teubner Foodfoto JmbH

Recipes: Teubner Foodfoto JmbH and
Lynda Zuber Sassi

Printed in China

ISBN: 1-59637-021-1

CONTENTS

INTRODUCTION

LEAVE IT TO THE ITALIANS to devise countless ways to indulge in bread. Since the beginning, bread has been a cornerstone of the Italian dining experience. *Panini* focuses on the Italian obsession of finding creative ways to savor one of their dietary and cultural staples—bread.

THIS BOOK EXPLORES the little caffè sandwiches of Italy, Tramezzini. They're the perfect afternoon pick me up. Heartier panini, Italian sandwiches, provide a tasty lunch whether you're on the go or have time to sit and relish in the flavors that are packed between the crusty bread. The chapters on Crostini and Bruschetta explore the art of making the perfect open face canapé or appetizer to serve your guests with cocktails or before a meal.

WHEN PREPARING TO MAKE any of the recipes in this book, remember one thing: the better the quality and the fresher the ingredients, the better your result will be. Think of this when you are choosing bread and selecting the ingredients that will go inside or on top of it. Typical to Italian cooking, the freshest and most seasonal ingredients are the focal point of any meal. Use a minimum of ingredients and let their freshness speak.

BEGIN WITH THE QUALITY of the bread. Go to an Italian bakery and discover the range of shapes and flavors. Or, make your own bread at home for guaranteed freshness. What matters most is that the bread is as fresh as it can be.

CHOOSE INGREDIENTS SEASONALLY. Think of the combination of mouth-watering ingredients such as sweet crusty Italian bread, fruity olive oil, fresh mozzarella, thinly sliced Italian cold cuts, and ripe, sweet, red tomatoes. The classic Tomato and Basil Crostini is divine in the summertime with a tomato plucked from the back yard and freshly snipped basil leaves. Likewise, in winter, the Black Olive Tapinade Crostini is the perfect choice.

TRAMEZZINI

CROSTINI

BRUSCHETTA

PANINI

IN RECENT YEARS, the panini press has become a must have kitchen tool. Yours can be used for most of the recipes in this book. Since instructions vary between manufacturers, be sure to become familiar with the ins and outs of your press prior to using.

IF YOU HAVEN'T TAKEN THE PLUNGE and purchased a panini press, you can still enjoy the recipes in this book. Just grill the bread in the oven under the broiler, on a griddle, in a pan on the stovetop, on the barbecue grill, or pop it in the toaster.

THE SIMPLICITY AND VARIETY of *Panini* will shed new light on bread as a focal part of the Italian dining experience. As you experiment with the recipes in this book, be creative. Toast a panini freddo, turn a crostini into a bruschetta and vice versa, substitute different types of fresh breads, and experiment with extra virgin olive oil flavors. After all, panini, tramezzini, crostini, and bruschetta are whatever you want them to be!

TRAMEZZINI

TRAMEZZINI ARE THE LITTLE CAFFÈ SANDWICHES of Italy. They are thin and filled with purées, pâtés, slices of meat, vegetables, or cheese. Tramezzini are eaten in the late afternoon as a snack accompanied by a glass of wine or an aperitif. Lately, they have also become popular to eat for lunch at trendy sidewalk caffès.

The bread typically used for tramezzini is *pane in cassetta*, which is the equivalent of our sandwich bread. Usually, the crust is removed and the sandwich is cut into two or four neat little triangles.

It is important to use the highest quality white or wheat bread that is either found at a bakery or that you make yourself. The bread should be made with unbleached, all-purpose flour and free of additives and preservatives. If it is not already, slice the loaf thinly and remove the crust before assembling.

As a variation, tramezzini recipes in this chapter can be grilled or toasted.

Roast Beef

Tramezzini

1 tbs softened butter
1 tsp horseradish
10 slices high quality wheat
    sandwich bread
10 slices roast beef (about ⅓ lb;
    or substitute turkey breast)
½ cup mayonnaise
½ cup plain yogurt
1 orange, peeled and chopped
½ bunch chives, chopped
Kosher salt
Freshly ground pepper

IN A BOWL, combine butter and horseradish and spread onto 5 slices of bread. Arrange 1 slice of roast beef on top of each of the 5 slices.

IN ANOTHER BOWL, combine mayonnaise, yogurt, orange, and chives and season to taste with salt and pepper. Spread onto the remaining 5 slices of bread then cover the roast beef. Press down gently and cut diagonally into halves or quarters.

MAKES 20 TRAMEZZINI

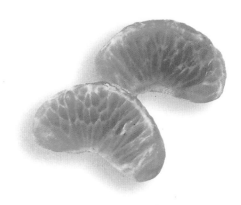

Chicken and Melon Tramezzini

2 chicken breast fillets (about
⅓ lb each)
1 tsp lemon zest
2 tsp hot mustard, separated
2 tbs olive oil
1 bunch arugula, chopped
1 cantaloupe or honeydew
melon, thinly sliced
1 tsp lemon juice
½ cup crème fraîche
10 slices high quality white
sandwich bread
Kosher salt
Freshly ground pepper

SEASON CHICKEN with salt and pepper. Combine lemon zest and 1 teaspoon of mustard and rub into the chicken.

IN A PAN, heat oil and sauté chicken over medium heat for 5 minutes on each side until thoroughly cooked. Let cool, then cut into thin slices.

IN A BOWL, combine arugula and melon and drizzle with lemon juice. Stir in crème fraîche and remaining mustard and season to taste with salt and pepper.

ARRANGE HALF of the arugula and melon onto 5 slices of bread, followed by the chicken, and the second half of the arugula and melon. Cover with the remaining bread, press down gently, cut in half diagonally, and serve.

THESE TRAMEZZINI are also delicious if you substitute cucumber or mango for the melon.

MAKES 20 TRAMEZZINI

Tramezzini
del Gambero

½ lb raw shrimp
1 tomato, seeded and diced
½ cup basil, chopped
½ cup mayonnaise
1 ripe avocado, thinly sliced
1 tbs lemon juice
4 lettuce leaves
10 slices high quality wheat
    sandwich bread
Kosher salt
Freshly ground pepper

DEVEIN THE SHRIMP by making a shallow cut lengthwise on the back curve of the shell. Discard the black vein and rinse under cold water. Cook shrimp in boiling, salted water for 1–2 minutes until they turn pink. Drain and cool. Once cool, dice into small pieces.

IN A BOWL, combine shrimp, tomato, basil, and mayonnaise. Season to taste with salt and pepper.

DRIZZLE AVOCADO slices with lemon juice.

TO ASSEMBLE: Evenly divide shrimp, avocado, and lettuce onto 5 pieces of bread. Cover with remaining bread, press down gently, and cut in half diagonally. Serve immediately so the avocado doesn't discolor.

MAKES 20 TRAMEZZINI

Roasted Red Pepper and Goat Cheese Tramezzini

3 roasted red bell peppers, chopped
1 small red onion, chopped
1 tbs chopped thyme leaves
5 oz goat cheese
18 slices high quality white
    sandwich bread
6 small lettuce leaves
Kosher salt
Freshly ground pepper
Toothpicks (optional)

COMBINE RED PEPPERS, onion, thyme, and goat cheese and season to taste with salt and pepper. Rinse lettuce leaves and dry.

TOAST THE BREAD and remove the crust. Spread half of the goat cheese onto 6 slices of bread, cover with 6 more slices of bread, and place 1 lettuce leaf on top. Spread remaining goat cheese on remaining bread and cover the lettuce. Press down gently and cut in half diagonally.

MAKES 24 TRAMEZZINI

Roasted Vegetable and Mozzarella Tramezzini

1 yellow bell pepper, cut into strips
1 bunch green onions, green ends
   removed and quartered
1 medium carrot, cut into strips
½ zucchini, thinly sliced
2 tbs olive oil
1 tsp lemon juice
4½ oz mozzarella
½ cup basil, chopped
½ cup mayonnaise
2 cloves garlic, minced
10 slices high quality white or
   whole-wheat sandwich bread
Kosher salt
Freshly ground pepper

PREHEAT OVEN BROILER. In a bowl, combine vegetables, olive oil, lemon juice, salt, and pepper and spread on a baking sheet. Broil for 10–12 minutes, turning occasionally, until the vegetables are brown and tender.

DRAIN MOZZARELLA and cut into thin slices. In a bowl, combine basil, mayonnaise, and garlic.

TO ASSEMBLE: Spread garlic mayonnaise onto 5 slices of the bread. Top with vegetables and mozzarella. Cover with remaining bread, press down gently, and cut in half diagonally.

MAKES 20 TRAMEZZINI

Tramezzini della Melanzana

1 eggplant
½ cup ricotta cheese
2–3 tbs olive oil
½ yellow bell pepper, cut into strips
½ red bell pepper, cut into strips
1 zucchini, thinly sliced
1 yellow onion, sliced
1 tsp chopped thyme leaves
8 slices high quality white or
    whole-wheat sandwich bread
8 oz mozzarella di bufala,
    thinly sliced
2 tbs chopped basil
Kosher salt
Freshly ground pepper

BAKE EGGPLANT IN A 450° oven for 30–40 minutes until tender. Slice in half, remove flesh, and purée with ricotta. Season with salt and pepper and set aside.

IN A LARGE PAN, heat oil and sauté bell peppers, zucchini, and onions over moderate heat for 4–5 minutes. Add thyme and season with salt and pepper.

TO ASSEMBLE: Spread eggplant on all slices of the bread. Arrange vegetables and mozzarella on 4 slices and sprinkle basil on top. Cover with remaining slices, press together gently, and cut in half diagonally.

MAKES 16 TRAMEZZINI

Tramezzini
con Fagioli

5 oz canned, cooked white beans
   (or garbanzo beans)
½ cup plain yogurt
½ lemon
1 clove garlic, minced
½ cup basil, chopped
1 tbs olive oil
10 slices high quality whole-wheat
   sandwich bread
10 thin slices prosciutto
15 cucumber slices
Kosher salt
Freshly ground pepper

DRAIN BEANS and purée with yogurt until smooth. Zest the lemon and then squeeze the juice. Add lemon zest and juice, garlic, basil, and olive oil to the bean purée. Season generously with salt and pepper.

TO ASSEMBLE: Spread the bean spread onto 5 slices of bread. Top with prosciutto and cucumber. Cover with remaining bread, press down gently, and slice diagonally.

MAKES 20 TRAMEZZINI

CROSTINI

CROSTINI ARE THIN SLICES OF BREAD, brushed with olive oil and lightly toasted in the oven then topped with a variety of ingredients, ranging from spreadable tomato purée to chunkier toppings like smoked salmon or tuna.

Crostini are ideal snacks and appetizers. They can be dressed up or down. You may choose to make just one kind or several so your guests can enjoy the options. For a more robust snack or appetizer offering, add a platter of cold cuts, including prosciutto, salami, and mortadella to your crostini platter.

Fettunta

½ cup softened butter
6 garlic cloves, minced
1 bunch parsley, chopped
Pinch of cayenne pepper
1 tsp dry sherry
1 baguette
Kosher salt
Freshly ground pepper

IN A FOOD PROCESSOR, combine butter, garlic, parsley, cayenne, and sherry. Season with salt and pepper. Mix together until smooth then refrigerate.

PREHEAT OVEN TO 400°F. Slice baguette crosswise at 1 inch intervals without cutting all the way through. Spread the butter between the slices. Wrap baguette in aluminum foil and bake in the oven for 15 minutes.

MAKES 1 BAGUETTE

Creative Crostini

1 fresh baguette
2–3 tbs high-quality extra
    virgin olive oil
Kosher salt

Toppings
Red pepper flakes
Chopped parsley
Chopped basil
Roasted garlic
Tapinade
Flavor-infused olive oil

PREHEAT OVEN BROILER.
Cut baguette in ½ inch slices
crosswise. Arrange bread on a
baking sheet and grill under
a broiler until golden brown.
Remove from the oven and
drizzle with olive oil and
sprinkle with a little salt.

CHOOSE YOUR FAVORITE
toppings from the list and
sprinkle on top.

MAKES 1 BAGUETTE

Crostini Classico

2 Roma tomatoes, seeds removed
    and chopped
2 tbs chopped basil
2 tsp capers
2 cloves garlic, peeled
½ cup olive oil, separated
8 slices sourdough baguette
Kosher salt
Freshly ground black pepper
Basil leaves for garnish

IN A BOWL, combine tomatoes, basil, capers, garlic, and 2 tablespoons of olive oil. Season to taste with salt and pepper.

PREHEAT OVEN BROILER. Place bread on a baking sheet and drizzle olive oil on each slice. Grill under the broiler until golden. Spread tomatos on the bread and garnish with basil leaves.

MAKES 8 CROSTINI

Crostini del Pomodoro

1 beefsteak tomato, seeded
    and chopped
½ cup extra virgin olive
    oil, separated
2 large cloves garlic, minced
8 slices sourdough baguette
    (about ½ inch thick)
Kosher salt
Freshly ground pepper

IN A BOWL, combine tomato with 2 tablespoons of olive oil and garlic. Season to taste with salt and pepper.

PREHEAT OVEN BROILER. Place bread on a baking sheet and drizzle each slice with remaining olive oil. Grill in the oven until golden. Spread tomatoes evenly on each slice of bread.

MAKES 8 CROSTINI

Crostini with Black Olive Tapinade

⅔ cup pitted black olives
½ cup capers, drained
2 oz anchovy fillets in oil, drained
1 clove garlic
⅓ cup olive oil, separated
1 fresh baguette
15 pimento-stuffed green olives
Freshly ground pepper

IN A BLENDER, combine olives, capers, anchovies, garlic, and 2 tablespoons of olive oil. Blend until the ingredients form a smooth paste. Transfer to a bowl and season to taste with pepper.

PREHEAT OVEN BROILER. Slice the baguette crosswise into about 15 slices. Place on a baking sheet and grill under the broiler until golden. Spread the tapinade generously on each slice. Cut the green olives in half and place 1 on top of each piece of crostini.

MAKES 15 CROSTINI

Smoked Trout Crostini

½ cup cream cheese
1 tsp lemon juice
2 tbs chopped dill
8 baguette slices (½ inch thick)
2 tbs olive oil
½ lb smoked trout, sliced
    into 8 pieces
8 small sprigs dill
2 thin lemon slices, cut
    into quarters
Kosher salt
Freshly ground pepper

IN A BOWL, combine cream cheese, lemon juice, and dill. Season to taste with salt and pepper.

PREHEAT OVEN BROILER. Place baguette slices on a baking sheet and drizzle with olive oil. Grill under the broiler until golden. Spread cream cheese on each slice of bread and top with a slice of trout, a sprig of dill, and a slice of lemon.

MAKES 8 CROSTINI

Smoked Salmon Crostini

½ lb smoked salmon, unsliced
1 tsp lemon juice
2 green onions, chopped
½ cup cream cheese
2 tbs chopped chives
8 slices sweet baguette or ciabatta
    (½ inch thick)
2 tbs olive oil
Kosher salt
Freshly ground pepper

RINSE THE SALMON, pat dry, and dice. In a bowl, combine salmon, lemon juice, onions, and season with salt and pepper. Cover and let stand for 10 minutes.

IN ANOTHER BOWL, combine cream cheese and chives. Stir until smooth.

PREHEAT OVEN BROILER. Place the baguette slices on a baking sheet and drizzle with olive oil. Grill under the broiler until golden. Remove from the oven and spread cream cheese on each slice then top with salmon. Sprinkle with extra chopped chives.

MAKES 8 CROSTINI

Crostini del Tonno

2 red bell peppers, roasted
    and chopped
3 green onions, cut into rings
1 can tuna packed in oil
2 tsp capers, chopped
¼ cup black olives, chopped
3 tsp lemon juice
16 slices sourdough baguette
½ cup olive oil
Kosher salt
Freshly ground pepper

IN A BOWL, combine red bell
peppers, onions, tuna (including
oil), capers, olives, and lemon
juice. Season to taste with salt
and pepper.

PREHEAT OVEN BROILER.
Place baguette slices on a baking
sheet and drizzle with olive oil.
Grill under the broiler until golden.
Remove from the oven and scoop
tuna onto each piece.

MAKES 16 CROSTINI

BRUSCHETTA

ONE OF THE GREAT, CLASSIC DISHES OF ITALY, bruschetta crosses all seasons and is adaptable to a wide range of toppings. The foundation of bruschetta is a large piece of crusty Italian bread grilled, then rubbed with garlic, drizzled with high quality extra virgin olive oil, and sprinkled with a little sea salt and maybe some pepper. Bruschetta are typically larger and more filling than crostini.

Usually bruschetta is served as an appetizer or first course, but stacked with fresh, quality ingredients it can also be enjoyed as a hearty open face sandwich. The options for toppings are endless ranging from a classic chopped tomato and basil to something less traditional like avocadoes.

Bruschetta Rustica

3–4 Roma tomatoes, seeded
    and diced
1 yellow onion, diced
3 sprigs rosemary, leaves removed
    and chopped
4 slices crusty Italian bread
2 garlic cloves, peeled and cut
    in half
½ cup olive oil
Kosher salt
Freshly ground pepper

IN A BOWL, combine tomatoes, onions, and rosemary. Season to taste with salt and pepper.

GRILL OR TOAST both sides of the bread until golden brown. Rub each slice with garlic, brush with remaining olive oil, and sprinkle with salt and pepper. Arrange the tomatoes evenly on top of the toast and garnish with rosemary.

MAKES 4 BRUSCHETTA

Gorgonzola Bruschetta

2–3 Roma tomatoes, chopped
½ cup red onions, sliced into rings
½ cup olive oil, separated
8 slices crusty Italian baguette
2 garlic cloves, peeled and cut
    in half
2 oz Gorgonzola, crumbled
1 tsp chopped basil
Kosher salt
Freshly ground pepper

IN A BOWL, combine tomatoes, onions, and 2 tablespoons of olive oil. Season to taste with salt and pepper.

PREHEAT OVEN BROILER. Grill or toast bread on both sides until golden brown. Rub each slice with garlic, brush with remaining olive oil, and sprinkle with salt and pepper. Top with tomatoes, onions, and Gorgonzola. Place under the broiler until the Gorgonzola melts. Garnish with basil before serving.

MAKES 8 BRUSCHETTA

Bruschetta with Tomatoes and Anchovies

2–3 Roma tomatoes, diced
2 tbs white onions, chopped
½ cup olive oil, separated
5 oz goat cheese
1 tbs chopped basil
8 slices crusty Italian baguette
2 garlic cloves, peeled and sliced
    in half
8 anchovy fillets
Kosher salt
Freshly ground pepper

IN A BOWL, combine tomatoes, onions, 2 tablespoons of olive oil, and season with salt and pepper.

IN A BOWL, combine goat cheese and basil until smooth.

GRILL OR TOAST BREAD on both sides until golden brown. Rub each slice with garlic, brush with remaining olive oil, and sprinkle with salt and pepper. Spread the goat cheese on each piece of bread and top with tomatoes. Arrange one anchovy decoratively on top of each bruschetta.

MAKES 4 BRUSCHETTA

Bruschetta

con Prosciutto

1 zucchini, thinly sliced
½ cup olive oil, separated
8 slices crusty Italian baguette
2 garlic cloves, peeled and cut
   in half
2–3 Roma tomatoes, sliced
8 pieces prosciutto
4 slices provolone cheese, cut
   in half
Hungarian sweet paprika
2 sprigs parsley
Kosher salt
Freshly ground pepper

IN A PAN, heat 1 tablespoon of oil and sauté zucchini 3–4 minutes. Season with salt and pepper, then drain on paper towels.

PREHEAT OVEN BROILER. Grill or toast both sides of the bread until golden brown. Rub each slice with garlic, brush with remaining olive oil, and sprinkle with salt and pepper. Arrange tomatoes, zucchini, prosciutto, and provolone on each slice of bread. Sprinkle paprika over the top. Place under the broiler until provolone melts. Garnish with parsley.

MAKES 8 BRUSCHETTA

Bruschetta

con Funghi

3 tbs olive oil, separated
3 garlic cloves, 2 minced, 1 whole
8 oz large white mushrooms, sliced
2 tbs sherry
1 tbs chopped Italian parsley
¼ cup heavy cream
4 slices crusty Italian bread
2 slices prosciutto, cut in half
8 slices Roma tomato
4 slices medium-aged Gouda
½ bunch chives, finely chopped
Kosher salt
Freshly ground white pepper

IN A PAN, heat 2 tablespoons of oil and sauté garlic until it begins to let off some of its aroma. Add mushrooms, sherry, and parsley. Sauté until mushrooms begin to soften then add cream. Simmer for 5–7 minutes, stirring occasionally, and season to taste with salt and pepper.

PREHEAT OVEN BROILER. Grill or toast bread on both sides until golden brown. Rub one side of each piece of bread with garlic, brush with remaining olive oil, and sprinkle with salt and pepper. Top with mushrooms, prosciutto, tomatoes, and cheese. Place under the broiler until the cheese melts. Remove, sprinkle with chives, and serve.

MAKES 4 BRUSCHETTA

Grilled Vegetable Bruschetta

½ cup olive oil, separated
⅔ cup fennel, thinly sliced
⅓ cup zucchini, thinly sliced
1 small white onion, cut into rings
½ cup tomatoes, sliced
Pinch red pepper flakes
5 oz goat cheese
2 tbs heavy cream
2 tbs chopped black olives
1 tbs chopped fennel greens
8 slices crusty Italian baguette
2 garlic cloves, peeled and cut
   in half
Kosher salt
Freshly ground pepper

IN A PAN, heat 1 tablespoon of olive oil and sauté fennel for 4–5 minutes. Season with salt and pepper then remove. Add zucchini to the pan, sauté briefly on sides, season, and remove. Add 1 more tablespoon of olive oil and sauté onions until translucent. Add tomatoes and red pepper flakes, and sauté for 1 more minute.

IN A BOWL, combine the goat cheese, heavy cream, olives, and fennel greens until smooth. Season with salt and pepper.

GRILL OR TOAST both sides of the bread until golden brown. Rub each slice with garlic, brush with remaining olive oil, and sprinkle with salt and pepper. Arrange the grilled vegetables on top of each slice of bread and place a dollop of goat cheese on the side.

MAKES 8 BRUSCHETTA

Bruschetta con Gamberetti

½ cup olive oil, separated
4 medium raw shrimp, tails on
4 thin slices zucchini
4 yellow bell pepper rings
4 slices crusty Italian bread
2 garlic cloves, peeled and cut
   in half
7 oz feta cheese
1 Roma tomato, quartered
4 sprigs basil
Kosher salt
Freshly ground pepper

IN A PAN, heat 1 tablespoon olive oil and sauté shrimp until pink (about 3–4 minutes). Season with salt and pepper. Remove from the pan and let cool.

IN A PAN, heat 2 tablespoons of olive oil and sauté zucchini and yellow bell peppers. Season with salt and pepper. Remove from heat and set aside.

GRILL OR TOAST both sides of the bread until golden brown. Rub each slice with garlic, brush with remaining olive oil, and sprinkle with salt and pepper. Remove crust from the bread. Spread feta on each slice of bread, top with a tomato wedge, slice of zucchini, ring of yellow bell pepper, shrimp, and a sprig of basil. Grind fresh pepper over the top before serving.

MAKES 4 BRUSCHETTA

Bruschetta Verde

½ cup ricotta cheese
1 avocado, thinly sliced
½ tbs lime juice
3 tbs olive oil, separated
2 Roma tomatoes, seeds removed
    and chopped
2 tbs chopped onions
1 tbs chopped cilantro
½ cup vegetable oil
1 parsnip, thinly sliced
8 slices crusty Italian baguette
2 garlic cloves, peeled and cut
    in half
Kosher salt
Freshly ground pepper

IN A BOWL, combine ricotta, ½ of the avocado, and lime juice until smooth. Season with salt and pepper.

IN A BOWL, combine tomatoes, onions, cilantro, and 1 tablespoon of olive oil with a little salt.

IN A SAUCEPAN, heat the vegetable oil and deep-fry parsnip chips until golden. Remove with a slotted spoon, drain on paper towels, and sprinkle with a little salt.

GRILL OR TOAST both sides of the bread until golden brown. Rub each slice with garlic, brush with remaining olive oil, and sprinkle with salt and pepper.

TO ASSEMBLE: Spread cheese onto the bread, top with avocado slices, tomatoes, and parsnip chips. Garnish with additional cilantro.

MAKES 8 BRUSCHETTA

PANINI

IN ITALY, PANINI MEANS "SMALL BREAD." Traditionally this small bread was eaten as a light snack between meals. However, as work hours became longer and lunches became shorter, panini has become popular in the modern day as lunch. Likewise, in the US, panini have become the rage. Warm sandwiches and Italian style breads have added a cornucopia of new options to the otherwise staid deli bar.

Typically, panini brings visions of a warm, grilled, gooey, sandwich. What many people don't realize is that there are just as many cold panini as there are grilled. This chapter is full of hot and cold, light and hardy, classic and contemporary panini recipes that are sure to please all audiences.

Turkey Panino

1 michette or sourdough
    sandwich roll
1 tbs mayonnaise
2 tbs mustard
4 slices turkey breast
3 slices tomato
6 slices cucumber
2 leaves red leaf lettuce

CUT ROLL IN HALF lengthwise and spread one side with mayonnaise and the other with mustard.

ARRANGE TURKEY, tomato, cucumber, and lettuce on top of one half and cover with the other. Press down gently, cut panino in half, and serve.

MAKES 1 PANINO

Turkey and Cranberry Panino

1 michette or sourdough
    sandwich roll
3 tbs cream cheese
1 tsp cranberry jelly
3 slices turkey breast
4 slices tomato
Spring lettuce mix

CUT ROLL IN HALF lengthwise. Combine the cream cheese and cranberry jelly until smooth and spread on both halves of the roll.

ARRANGE TURKEY, tomatoes, and lettuce on top of one half. Cover with the other half, press down gently, and cut panino in half.

MAKES 1 PANINO

Panino with Smoked Turkey

2 tsp butter
2 slices sunflower or other
    grain bread
3–4 slices smoked turkey breast
2 slices Swiss cheese
3 slices red bell pepper, roasted
2 red onion rings
Several arugula leaves

SPREAD BUTTER on both slices of the bread.

ARRANGE TURKEY, cheese, red bell peppers, onions, and arugula on one slice and cover with other. Grill in a panini press until golden brown or serve cold. Slice panino in half to serve.

MAKES 1 PANINO

Turkey and Cheese Panino

2 tsp mustard
2 slices fruit or nut bread
4 slices tomato
2 slices Havarti cheese
3 slices red bell pepper, roasted
2 red onion rings
4 basil leaves
2 slices smoked turkey
1 tbs olive oil
Kosher salt
Freshly ground pepper

SPREAD MUSTARD onto both slices of bread.

ARRANGE TOMATOES, Havarti, red bell peppers, onions, basil, and turkey on top of one slice of bread. Drizzle with olive oil and sprinkle with salt and pepper. Cover with the second slice of bread and grill in a panini press until golden or serve cold. Cut panino in half and serve.

MAKES 1 PANINO

Ham Panino

2 tbs sour cream
1 tbs cranberry jelly
2 slices oatmeal or
    whole-wheat bread
Assorted lettuce leaves
4 slices tomato
4 slices ham
Kosher salt
Freshly ground pepper

IN A BOWL, combine sour cream and cranberry jelly until smooth. Spread onto both slices of bread.

ARRANGE TOMATOES, lettuce, and ham on top of one slice of bread. Cover with the second slice and grill in a panini press until golden brown or serve cold.

CUT PANINO in half and serve with additional cranberry jelly on the side.

MAKES 1 PANINO

Roasted Duck Breast Panino

2 tsp butter
2 slices nut or fruit bread
1 tbs orange marmalade
2 oz sliced roast duck breast
2–3 radicchio leaves
1 tbs olive oil
Kosher salt
Freshly ground pepper

SPREAD BUTTER on one slice of bread and marmalade on the other.

ARRANGE DUCK and radicchio on top of the marmalade, drizzle with olive oil, and sprinkle with salt and pepper. Cover with the second slice of bread and grill in a panini press until golden brown or serve cold. Slice panino in half to serve.

MAKES 1 PANINO

Waldorf Salad Panino

1 tbs celery, diced
3 tbs apples, diced
2 tsp walnuts, chopped
1 tbs mayonnaise
2 slices whole-wheat bread
2 tsp butter
2 oz Bavarian blue cheese, sliced
2 slices ham
Kosher salt
Freshly ground pepper

IN A BOWL, combine celery, apples, walnuts, and mayonnaise. Season mixture to taste with salt and pepper.

GRILL BREAD in a panini maker or toaster. Spread butter on one slice of the bread and arrange blue cheese, ham, and salad on top. Cover with the second slice of bread, press down gently, and cut bread into quarters.

GARNISH TOP of paninio with additional chopped apples.

MAKES 1 PANINO

Black Forest Ham and Cheese Panino

2 slices whole-wheat bread
1 tbs mayonnaise
1 tsp Dijon mustard
2 slices Black Forest ham
1 slice Swiss cheese
2 slices tomato
1 leaf Bibb lettuce

SPREAD MAYONNAISE onto one slice of bread and mustard on the other.

ARRANGE HAM, cheese, tomato, and lettuce on top of one slice. Cover with second slice. Grill in panini press until golden brown or serve cold. Slice panino in half before serving.

MAKES 1 PANINO

Ahi Tuna Panini

1 piece ahi tuna (4 oz)
1 tbs olive oil
2 slices crusty Italian bread
1 tbs mayonnaise
1 tbs Dijon mustard
Kosher salt
Freshly ground black pepper

SEASON the tuna with salt and pepper.

IN A PAN, heat the olive oil and sear the tuna on all sides.

SPREAD mayonnaise on one slice of the bread and mustard on the other. Place the tuna on one slice of bread and cover it with the other slice.

GRILL in a panini press until golden brown, then slice bread in half, and serve with a green salad.

MAKES 1 PANINI

BLT—Bacon, Lettuce, and Tomato Panino

4 slices bacon
1 tbs olive oil
1 tomato, sliced
2 slices white sandwich bread
2 tbs mayonnaise
4–6 arugula leaves
Kosher salt

IN A PAN, fry bacon until crispy.

DRIZZLE OLIVE OIL over sliced tomatoes and sprinkle with a little salt.

GRILL THE BREAD in a panini press or toaster. Spread mayonnaise on both slices of bread. Top one slice with pancetta, tomato, and tomato. Cover with the second slice, press down gently, and cut in half diagonally.

MAKES 1 PANINO

Ham and Blue Cheese Panino

1 tbs Dijon mustard
2 slices oatmeal or
    whole-wheat bread
2 slices ham
3 slices tomato
1 red onion ring
1 oz blue cheese
6 arugula leaves

SPREAD MUSTARD on both slices of bread.

ARRANGE HAM, tomatoes, onions, blue cheese, and arugula on one slice of bread. Cover with the second slice. Grill in a panini press until golden brown or serve cold. Slice panino in half before serving.

MAKES 1 PANINO

Double Decker
Italian Panino

3 slices whole-wheat or
    sourdough bread
1 tsp butter
1 tsp cranberry jelly
2 tbs cream cheese
3 slices ham
2 slices mortadella
6 slices cucumber
2 red onion rings

SPREAD ONE SLICE of bread with butter, the second slice with cranberry jelly, and the third slice with half of the cream cheese.

ARRANGE HAM on the slice of bread with butter, cover with the slice of bread with cranberry facing down, and spread the remaining cream cheese on top. Arrange the mortadella, cucumbers, and onions on top of the second slice of bread, and cover with the last slice, cream cheese facing down. Slice panino in half and serve.

MAKES 1 PANINO

Ham and
Chutney Panino

1 michette or sourdough roll
2 tsp butter
1–2 tbs onion-apple chutney
3 slices ham
2 slices tomato
Several arugula leaves

CUT ROLL in half. Spread butter and chutney on both halves.

ARRANGE HAM, tomatoes, and arugula on one half and cover with the other. Slice panino in half and enjoy.

MAKES 1 PANINO

Prosciutto e Formaggio Panino

1 tbs olive oil
2 slices crusty Italian bread
3 slices prosciutto
2 slices cheddar cheese
Kosher salt

DRIZZLE OLIVE OIL on both slices of the bread. Place proscuitto and cheddar cheese on one slice of bread and cover with the second slice.

GRILL in a panini press until golden brown or serve cold. Slice panino in quarters before serving.

MAKES 1 PANINO

Salami, Cheese, and Pineapple Panino

2 slices crusty Italian bread
1 tsp butter
1 tbs pineapple jam or chutney
6 slices salami
2 red onion rings
1 slice Jack cheese
2 Bibb lettuce leaves
2 slices tomato
1 dill pickle

SPREAD BUTTER on one slice of bread and chutney on the other.

ARRANGE SALAMI, onions, provolone, lettuce, and tomatoes on top of the slice of bread with chutney. Cover with the second slice, butter facing down, and grill in a panini press until golden brown or serve cold. Slice panino in half to serve.

GARNISH with a thinly sliced pickle fanned out on top of the panino.

MAKES 1 PANINO

Italian Cold Cut Panino

1 crusty sourdough baguette
2 tsp sweet mustard
2 tbs olive oil
5 slices salami
3 slices capocolla
3 slices provolone cheese
2 slices tomato
2 tbs chopped chives
Kosher salt
Freshly ground pepper

CUT BAGUETTE in half lengthwise. Spread mustard on one side of the baguette and drizzle olive oil on the other.

ARRANGE SALAMI, capocolla, and provolone on top of the mustard side of the baguette. Sprinkle with salt and pepper, and then add tomatoes. Cover with the other half. Grill in a panini press until golden brown or serve cold. Slice panino in half to serve and garnish with chives.

MAKES 1 PANINO

Mortadella, Brie, and Avocado Panino

3 slices mortadella
½ avocado, sliced
2 oz Brie, sliced
1 tbs olive oil
2 slices whole-wheat bread
Cranberry jelly
Kosher salt
Freshly ground pepper

ARRANGE MORTADELLA, avocado, and Brie on top of one slice of bread. Drizzle with olive oil and sprinkle with salt and pepper. Cover with the second slice of bread, cut in half, and serve with additional avocado slices drizzled with olive oil, salt, and pepper.

SERVE IMMEDIATELY so that avocado doesn't discolor.

SERVE cranberry jelly on the side.

MAKES 1 PANINO

Open Faced

Pear Panino

1 large pear, cut in half
1 slice crusty wheat or white
    Italian bread
1 oz Gorgonzola, at
    room temperature
2 slices prosciutto
1 slice Gouda
½ tsp chopped Italian parsley

PREHEAT OVEN BROILER. Cut
pear lengthwise into a fan shape.

GRILL THE BREAD in a panini
press or under the broiler. Spread
the Gorgonzola on the toasted
bread, followed by the pears,
prosciutto, and Gouda. Place
under the broiler for 3–4 minutes.
Remove once the Gouda begins
to melt. Sprinkle with parsley
before serving.

MAKES 1 PANINO

Hamburger Panini

1 clove garlic, minced
1 green onion, chopped
½ bunch Italian parsley, chopped
½ lb ground beef
1 egg
Pinch of paprika
1 tbs olive oil
2 zucchinis, thinly sliced
⅓ cup crème fraîche
1 tbs ketchup
4 baguette or michette rolls
8 Bibb lettuce leaves
2 tomatoes, sliced
Kosher salt
Freshly ground pepper

IN A BOWL, combine garlic, green onion, parsley, ground beef, egg, paprika, salt, and pepper. Shape into 4 rectangular patties. In a frying pan, fry the patties for 3–4 minutes on each side.

IN A PAN, heat the oil and sauté the zucchini until tender. Remove and set aside.

IN A BOWL, combine crème fraîche and ketchup, season with salt and pepper.

CUT ROLLS in half lengthwise and grill them under the broiler or in a panini press. Spread dressing on both halves of the baguette. Arrange the lettuce, tomato, hamburger, and zucchini on the bottom half. Cover with the top half, press together gently, and serve.

MAKES 4 PANINI

Panino with Chicken and Herb Mayonnaise

½ cup mayonnaise
2 tsp chopped chives
3 tsp chopped parsley
3 tsp chopped basil
2 tsp chopped mint
2 slices sourdough bread
4 slices chicken breast
Kosher salt
Freshly ground pepper

COMBINE mayonnaise and herbs together until smooth. Season to taste with salt and pepper.

SPREAD 1 tablespoon of mayonnaise on each slice of bread. Arrange chicken on top of one slice and cover with the other. Grill in a panini press until golden brown. Slice panino in half before serving.

MAKES 1 PANINO

Italian Sausage Panino

1 Italian sausage
1 sour baguette or michette
2 tbs Dijon mustard
6 slices cucumber
4 slices red bell pepper, roasted
2 red onion slices
2 romaine lettuce leaf

IN A PAN, cook the sausage until it's warm throughout. Slice sausage in half.

CUT THE BAGUETTE in half lengthwise. Spread mustard on the bottom halves of the rolls. Arrange sausage, cucumber, red bell pepper, onions, and lettuce on top of the mustard and cover with the top half of the roll. Press together gently and slice panini in half before serving.

MAKES 1 PANINO

Pâtè Panini

4 slices fruit or nut bread
2 tsp butter
2 slices red bell pepper, roasted
2½ oz country pâtè
6 slices cucumber
2 slices red onion

SPREAD BUTTER on two slices of bread and arrange red bell peppers, pâtè, cucumbers, and onions on top. Place the remaining slices of bread on top.

GRILL in a panini press until golden brown or serve cold. Slice panini in half before serving.

MAKES 2 PANINI

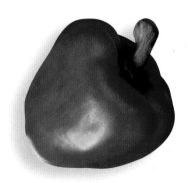

Panino del Formaggio

4 slices tomato
1 tbs olive oil
2 slices mozzarella
2 slices crusty Italian bread
Kosher salt

DRIZZLE OLIVE OIL over the tomatoes and sprinkle with a little salt.

ARRANGE mozzarella and tomatos on one slice of bread and cover with the other slice. Grill in a panini press or in a pan on the stove top until golden. Slice in half and serve with French fries and a green salad.

GARNISH with chopped parsley.

MAKES 1 PANINO

Spinach and
Cheese Panino

1 tbs mayonnaise
2 slices raisin or other fruit bread
4 slices Granny Smith apple
2–3 slices Gruyère cheese
Several young spinach leaves

SPREAD MAYONNAISE on both slices of bread.

ARRANGE the apples, Gruyère, and spinach on one slice of bread and cover with the other slice. Grill in a panini press until golden brown or serve cold. Slice panino in half before serving.

MAKES 1 PANINO

Panino with Brie and Hazelnuts

2 slices whole-wheat bread
1 tsp butter
Handful of mâche
2 oz Brie, sliced
2 tsp chopped hazelnuts

SPREAD BUTTER on both slices of bread.

ARRANGE MÂCHE and Brie on top of one slice. Sprinkle hazelnuts on top of the Brie and cover with the second slice. Cut panino in half to serve.

MAKES 1 PANINO

Cheese and Arugula Panini

1 sourdough baguette or
   michette roll
4–6 arugula leaves
2 slices provolone
1 tbs olive oil
Kosher salt

SLICE BAGUETTE in half
lengthwise.

ARRANGE CHEESE and arugula
in the middle. Drizzle with olive oil
and sprinkle with salt.

MAKES 1 PANINO

Vegetarian Panino

2 slices light rye bread
3 tsp cream cheese
6 paper-thin slices fennel
3 slices tomato
2 red onion rings
2 slices red bell pepper, roasted
Several young spinach leaves
1 tbs olive oil
2 tsp balsamic vinegar
Kosher salt
Freshly ground pepper

SPREAD CREAM CHEESE on top of both slices of bread.

ARRANGE FENNEL, tomatoes, onions, red bell peppers, and spinach on top. Drizzle with olive oil and vinegar and sprinkle with salt and pepper. Cover with the second slice of bread and grill in a panini press until golden brown or serve cold. Cut panino in half to serve.

MAKES 1 PANINO

Ham and
Cheese Panino

1 michette or sourdough
    sandwich roll
1 tbs mayonnaise
2 slices prosciutto
1 slice provolone
1 red onion ring
2 slices tomato
Several assorted lettuce leaves
Kosher salt

CUT THE ROLL IN HALF. Spread mayonnaise on both halves of the roll.

ROLL UP HAM AND PROVOLONE and stack on the bottom half of the roll followed by onions, tomatoes, and lettuce. Cover with the top half of the roll.

SLICE PANINO IN HALF before serving.

MAKES 1 PANINO

Smoked Salmon

Panino

1 sourdough baguette
2 tbs cream cheese
1 tbs chopped dill
2 green leaf lettuce leaves
3 oz smoked salmon
Juice from ½ lemon
Kosher salt
Freshly ground pepper

IN A BOWL, combine cream cheese and dill until creamy.

CUT THE ROLL IN HALF and spread the cream cheese on the bottom. Arrange lettuce and salmon and drizzle with lemon juice and sprinkle with salt and pepper. Cover with the top of the baguette.

GRILL IN A PANINI PRESS until golden.

MAKES 1 PANINO

Ham with Ginger Chutney Panino

1 tbs ginger chutney
2 slices sourdough or fruit bread
3 slices red bell pepper, roasted
2 slices tomato
1 red lettuce leaf
2 slices ham
1 tbs olive oil
Kosher salt
Freshly ground pepper

SPREAD GINGER CHUTNEY on one slice of bread.

ARRANGE RED BELL PEPPERS, tomatoes, lettuce, and ham on top of the slice with ginger chutney. Drizzle with olive oil and sprinkle with salt and pepper. Cover with the second slice of bread and grill in a panini press until golden brown or serve cold.

SLICE PANINO in half before serving.

MAKES 1 PANINO

INDEX